50 HOURS

A friend is having a baby, her first baby, at home with midwives—just 2½ minutes from the finest hospitals in Boston.

She is afraid of hospitals and hurried doctors who cut unnecessarily. She is birthing without drugs after nine months of eating fruit and grains and eggs and milk.

50 HOURS

Text by Dorothea Lynch • Photographs by Eugene Richards

Many Voices Press

For Tom Fitzgerald and Eileen Richardson.

Thanks to Jim Lukoski, Elizabeth Hamlin, and Donald Dietz.

Design by Eugene Richards.
Production by Katy Homans.
Printing by Rappoport Printing Corp.

LC 83-62239
ISBN 0-394-62023-2

Distributed by Grove Press, Inc.

50 HOURS was supported by a grant
from the John Simon Guggenheim Memorial Foundation.

From time to time Gene telephones, bored and weary.

"How's it going?"

"Slow. So damn slow. They're out cruising around Jamaica Pond."

I smile, imagining a long line of midwives, husband and friends following Marnie. Marnie in the long lace nightdress that had been her grandmother's birthing gown, stopping to let labor pains subside while joggers and laughing dogs stream by.

"Goddammit, I might have known she'd pick today to have her kid."

Two weeks late, Marnie and Jeff's baby is about to be born on the eve of the Seabrook antinuclear demonstration. Gene has been assigned to photograph the protesters who will try to occupy and stop construction of a partly built nuclear power plant. But he wants just as much to record the first birth he has ever seen. He tells me to go home and try to sleep. He will stay up all Friday night photographing the birth, then join a group of us for the dawn ride to New Hampshire.

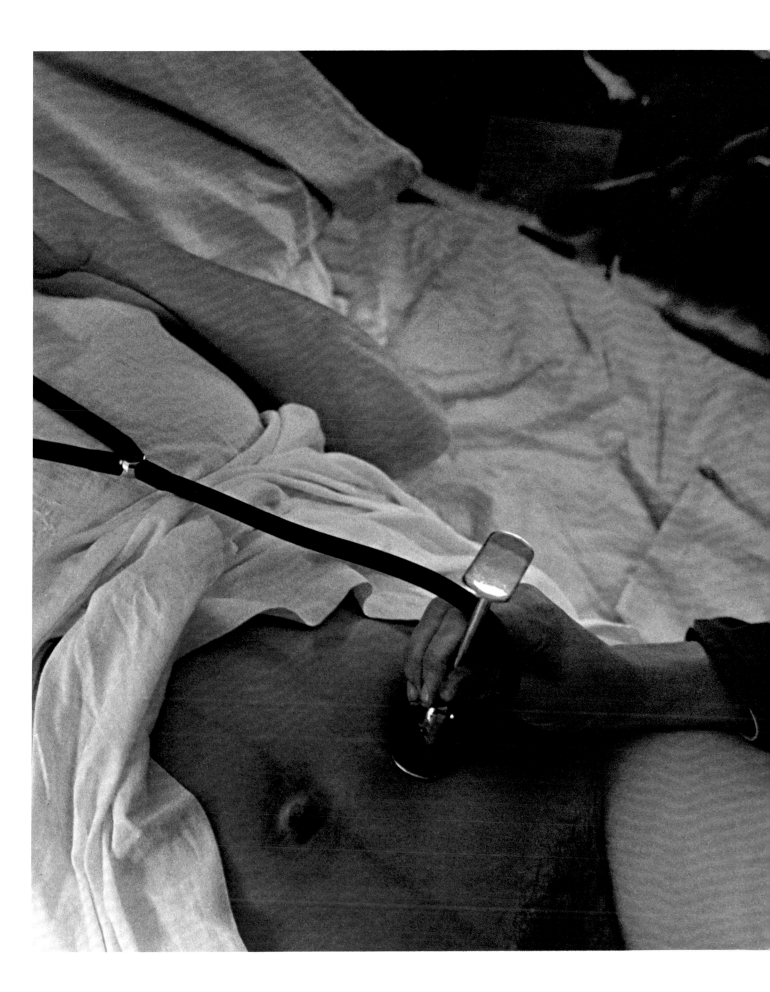

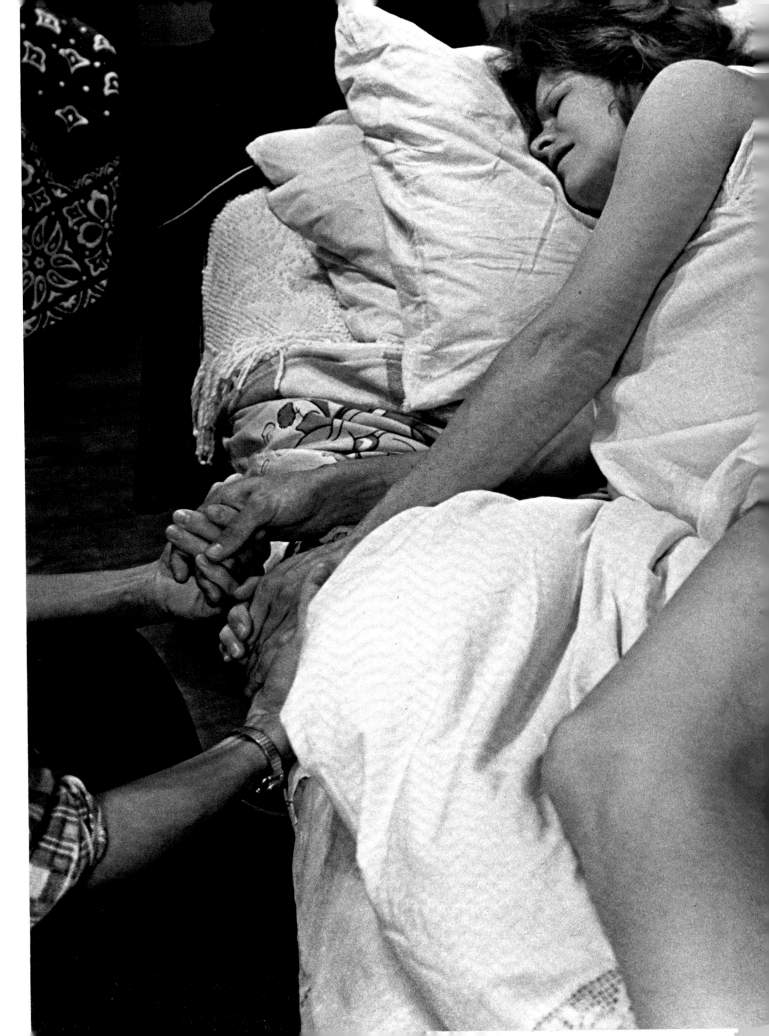

Assaults with mace and icy jets of high-powered water leave
the protesters and newsmen gasping and weeping, angry and
terrified. It is very difficult to run in the thick mud. And the

tidewaters are returning trapping us on isolated ground.

I can make out Gene coming towards me. Angry red welts
stain his forehead, neck and cheeks.

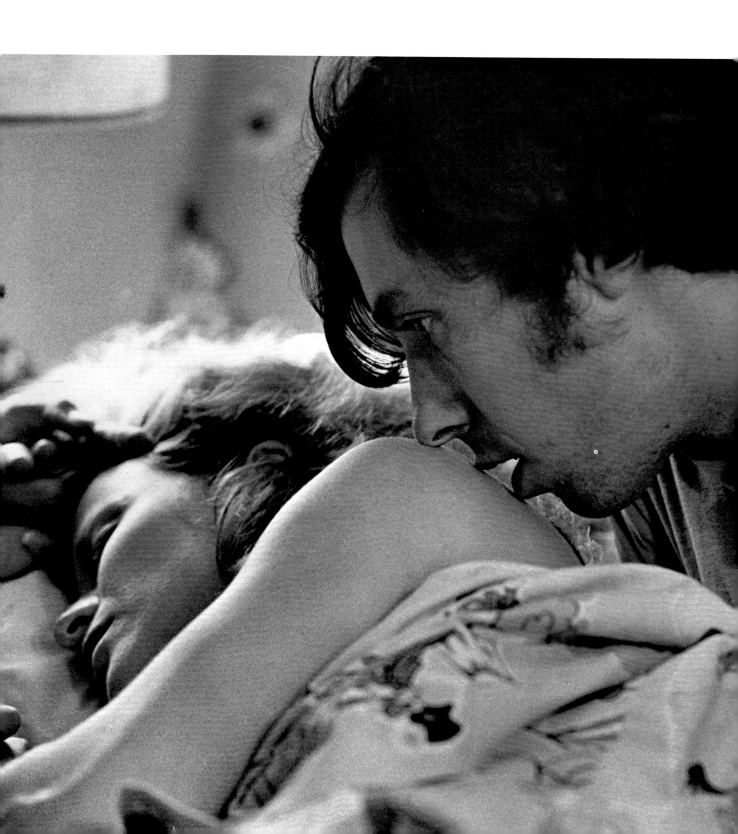

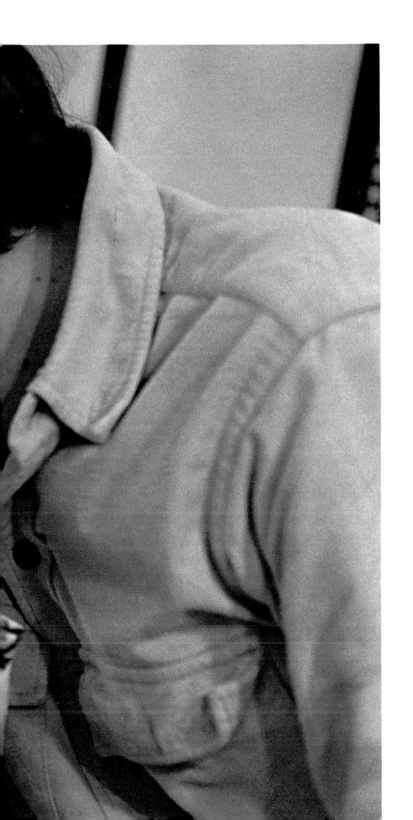

No baby all the long, long Saturday. Marnie's bedroom is warm and full of midwives, cats, hot compresses and the click of Gene's camera. It is almost luxurious to be one of so many people, all engaged in the same age-old task of birth.

Hospitals and doctors and birth defects might almost not
exist in this temporary world Marnie has created. During the
last nine months she has even stopped drinking caffeine and
alcohol, stopped eating pills and meats.

Her fears, rather than her ignorance, have created the old-fashioned climate. Her fears of a world filled with pollution and cancer, radiation, nuclear wastes, and wars blooming on every continent.

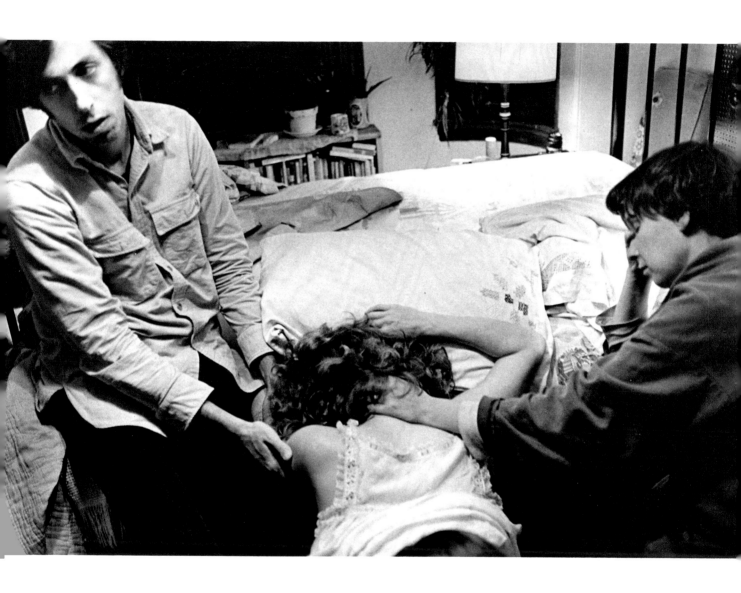

We take turns caressing Marnie's lustrous skin – the only
communication she is capable of receiving – and fall asleep one
by one in chairs, on the floor.

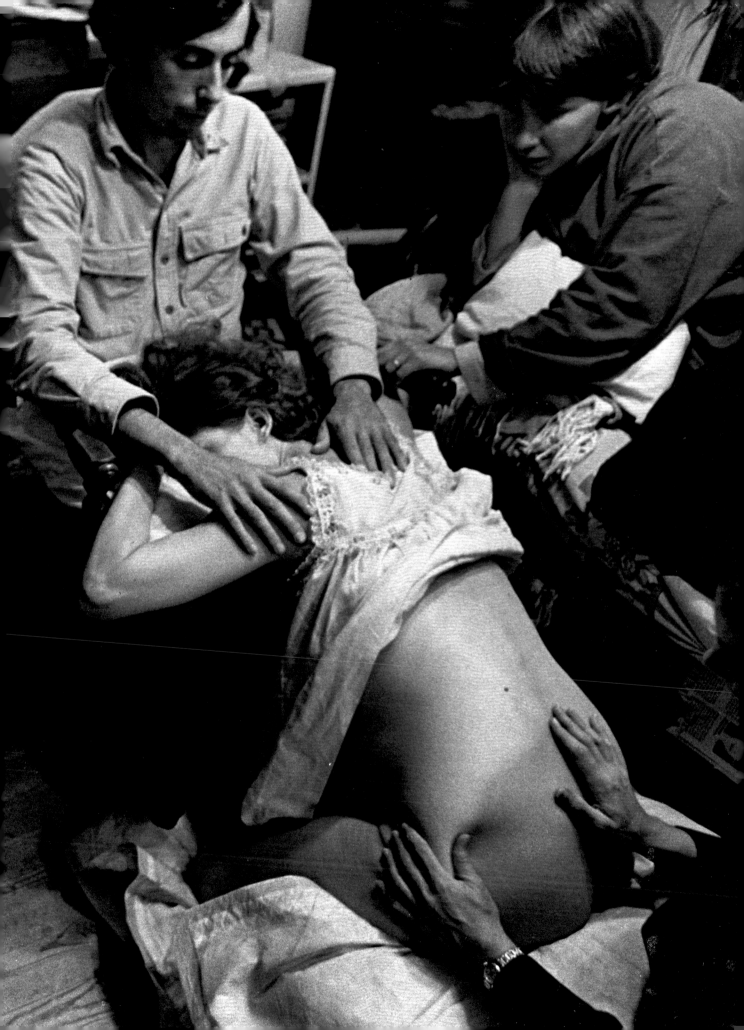

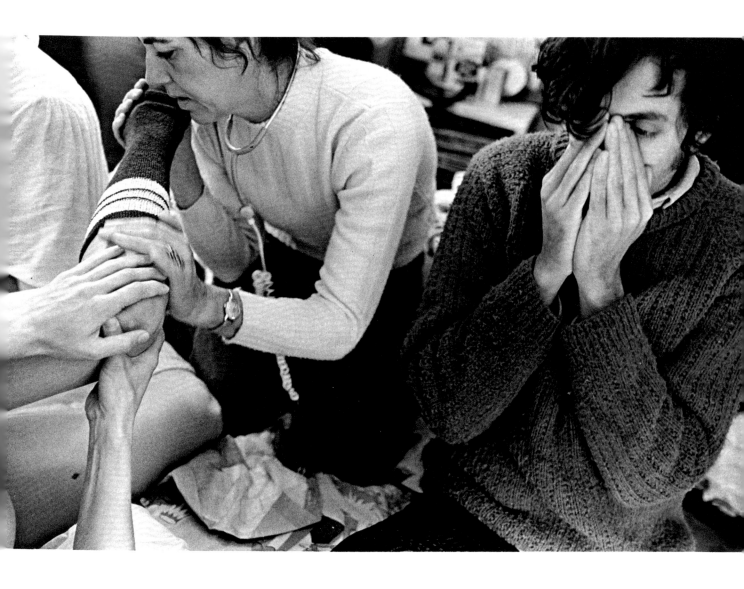

At 6:30 Sunday morning Marnie begins to scream, dragging
us back from dreams of shouting protesters.

And suddenly there it is. The convoluted, deep-wrinkled surface of another's body. The skull slips through.

It is a nightmare image, a demon, an exorcism. And suddenly it is much more than that, and less. Another person is swimming over into a new life.

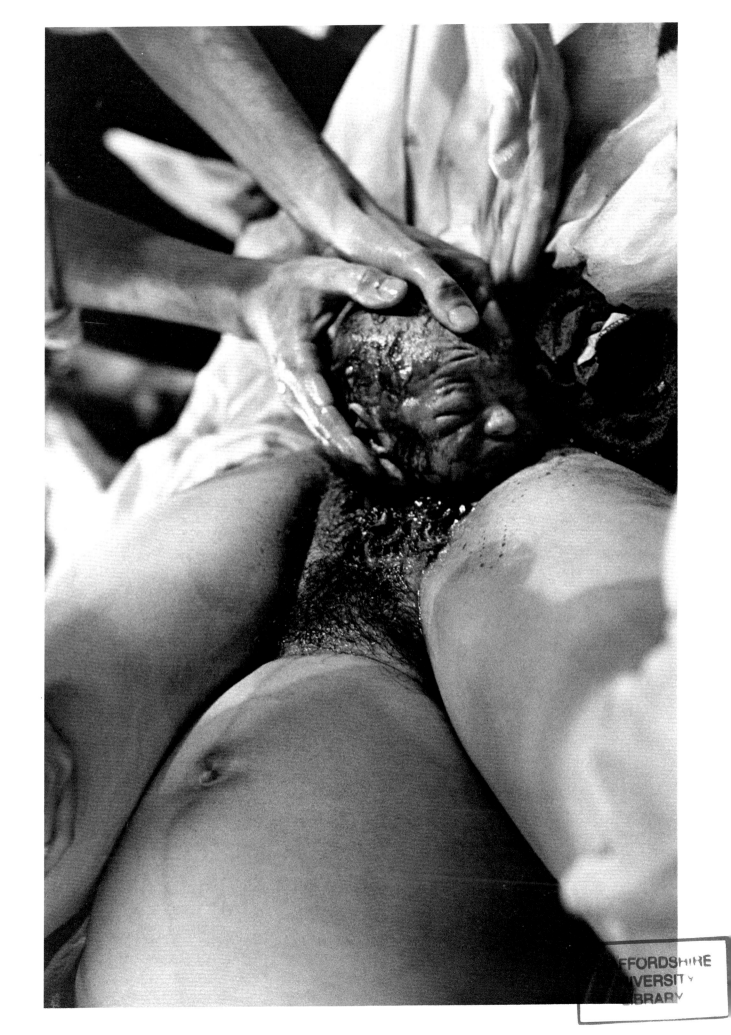

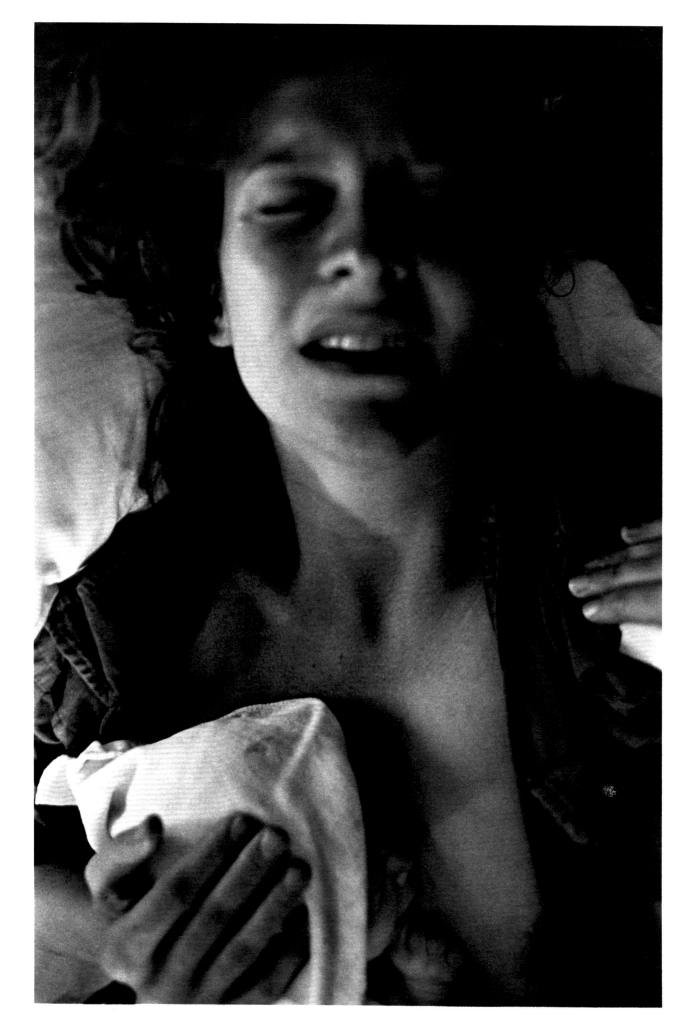

the sky in front of a line of demonstrators. Today, hundreds of small birds dip into the grass for nesting material. The marsh grass is golden and green, bending like a dancer before the pull of the wind. Moving above and below the colors are frogs, crickets, bees, newts, crabs, and silent, waiting fish.

A guy and a girl with pimples sprinkled over her cheeks stand before the main gate. They are the first protesters here, though it is late in the afternoon. In October they were everywhere, wearing ragpicker clothes, wool caps, hunting belts stuffed with granola and oranges and 5% boric acid solution to wash off the mace.

These two pass out leaflets to power plant employees who are getting into their cars. "A note to Seabrook Workers . . . Although many workers in the nuclear industry are aware of the dangers of nuclear power, many are hesitant to take a stand because they feel their jobs are threatened. However, the industry does not always benefit its workers. Nuclear workers are not considered members of the public, thus they are permitted to receive 30 times more radiation than the general public."

Most of the cars roll by with their windows up, drivers resolutely facing front.

"Get a job," someone shouts. Young people flash the old peace sign. One worker, waiting to pull into traffic, takes the flier.

"It's the only job I have," he says. "Find me another."

As night falls convoys of trucks carry in state police and guardsmen from Massachusetts, Rhode Island, Connecticut, Vermont and New Hampshire. Out in the moonlit fields tracks are being worn in the long grass, heading deep into the woods. We walk. No one talks. People with flashlights light up the ground at our feet so we can bypass twisted roots and streams on our way to the anti-nuke's camp.

There in the light from small fires men and women are sitting together in "affinity groups," role-playing; you-be-the-state-cop-and-I'll-be-the-good-person-going-all-out-for-America. They share the food they have brought with them, and speak of one another as new Americans, revolutionaries. But no one is friendly to us. The Clamshell Alliance, which has organized the demonstration, is wary of what they call the media.

The Clammers join arm and arm and begin to sing. It is like a girl scout camp. "Jesus," Jim says, disgusted. "Let's get out of here." The farther away from the campfires and the singing we walk, the louder are the sounds of the highway, the whine of truck tires on the pavement.

8 A.M. So much for going to the bathroom. It is difficult to concentrate when you share a motel room with men you don't know very well. Let alone when your stomach has come to the realization that you are going to a riot today.

Jim has trouble deciding which bowling shirt he should wear. "I have 27 of them. My mother finds them and sends them to me. You can't get shirts like this anymore." And Michael is upset because he has forgotten to bring along an ace bandage. He wants to tape up his chest to protect the fresh curved scars where the doctors worked to reinflate his collapsed lung.

K's Country House is crammed now with journalists and TV crews putting away coffee and big breakfasts for a long day. Being in Seabrook today suddenly seems a bad idea, trooping along to this demonstration, when I could probably see more on the six o'clock news. I remember last October's moments of panic as the tear gas blossomed and the protesters began running—me right along with them—and the police dogs pulled against their heavy chains.

Time to go. On the way out, Jim studies the photo of a nuclear power plant that's hanging next to the cash register.

"Oh, that's not a real picture," the manager assures us. "That's what they call a . . . a . . . model. To show what it's going to look like."

One of the regular customers looks at us and winks.

"Yup, that's what it looks like—before it starts to leak."

Just past noon the Clammers finally move out, into the fields leading to the nuclear power station fences. A cheer goes up. At the front of the line are men wearing face masks and carrying white shields with the letters NLF stencilled in red: Nuclear Liberation Force. Shades of Don Quixote, and Vietnam.

All of us are walking quickly—running through the long golden grass. How strange this is, how thrilling, not to know where I am going or what is ahead waiting, as if I am once more 16 years old on a spring day with my whole life stretching out in front of me.

Born in Dorchester, Mass. in 1944, Dorothea Lynch spent her life as a poet, waitress, social worker, newspaper correspondent and magazine writer. She wrote the postscript for **Dorchester Days,** and is the author of **Exploding Into Life** to be produced by Many Voices Press in 1984.

Photojournalist Eugene Richards, 39, is the author of **Few Comforts or Surprises: The Arkansas Delta,** and **Dorchester Days.** A member of Magnum Inc., he has been the recipient of grants from the Guggenheim Foundation, the W. Eugene Smith Memorial Fund and the National Endowment For The Arts.

Marnie Andrews, an actress and singer, and her husband Jeff Jacobson, a freelance photographer, live now on Staten Island with their son Henry Harry Whitener Jacobson.

Photograph by Jim Lukoski